For Women Only

Motorhome
Care & Maintenance

Margo Armstrong

The Maxwell Group Publishers

For Women Only: Motorhome Care & Maintenance

The authors and publisher have made their best effort to produce a high quality, informative and helpful book. They make no representation or warranties of any kind with regard to the completeness or accuracy of the contents of the book. They accept no liability of any kind for losses or damages caused or alleged to be caused, directly or indirectly, from using the information contained in this book.

ISBN: 978-0692772416

From the Author

The RV lifestyle, designed for having fun while traveling in comfort, does require care and maintenance. You are not having fun if the motorhome demands constant attention.

To keep your vehicle on the road and the driver happy, maintain good records and calendar future maintenance needs.

Following a few simple procedures in a timely manner keeps your older motorhome "looking new" and continues to keep that "look" for many happy years.

My twenty years of full-time experience and talking to others in the RV lifestyle has taught me an important lesson. The first motorhome dictates happiness or frustration, success or failure in this lifestyle. Take care of your vehicle and it takes care of you.

To help you reach your first goal, **download and complete** the *Motorhome Component Information* form. All the information about your rig is in one place, right at your fingertips when researching, ordering, upgrading, or buying parts.

TheRVLifestyle.MovingOnWithMargo.com#mh

See you down the road,

Margo

The RV Lifestyle Series: available at
Bookstores Worldwide:

Conquer the Road: RV Maintenance for Travelers
For Women Only: Traveling Solo in Your RV
How to Save Money While Enjoying the RV Lifestyle
Selling Online: Supporting the RV Lifestyle
Staying in Touch: A Traveler's Guide
The RV Lifestyle: A Dream Come True
Working on the Road: For Professionals and Just Fun-Loving Folks

Contents

Storing Your motorhome   **95**

Driving Tips   **97**

Introduction

The RV lifestyle, designed for having fun while traveling in comfort, does require care and maintenance. You are not having fun if the motorhome demands constant attention.

Following a few simple procedures in a timely manner can keep your older motorhome "looking new." With these same procedures, your new motorhome keeps that "look" for many happy years.

❖ Before the first trip, take the motorhome in for a complete service.

This service is more expensive than the annual and takes the longest time because you want everything checked including the axles, bearings and brakes.

❖ Even if brand new, quality control may have missed something vital when testing at the end of the manufacturing line.

❖ Vibration from rolling down the highway, hitting potholes and debris, and swaying in the wind are all factors to be considered. If right off the dealer's lot, that new motorhome possibly drove several thousand miles to get to your location.

❖ Once each year (or 3,000 miles) have the motorhome's oil and filter changed. This provides an opportunity for the service personnel to check all the liquids, look for leaks of any kind, make sure the tires are in good condition (more on this later), and generally look it over.

❖ Keep in mind that if the motorhome sits in storage for six to eight months out of the year, extra vigilance is needed (more on this later).

My twenty years of full-time experience and talking to others in the RV lifestyle have taught me an important lesson. The first motorhome dictates happiness or frustration, success or failure in this lifestyle. Take care of your vehicle and it takes care of you.

To help you reach your first goal, complete the *Motorhome Component Information* form. All the information about your rig is in one place, right at your fingertips when researching, ordering, upgrading, or buying parts.

To download the free PDF template for *"My Motorhome Component Information,"* and two other helpful forms, *"Checklist For The Road,"* and *"Onan Gas Genset Maintenance Schedule,"* please visit my webpage:

TheRVLifestyle.MovingOnWithMargo.com#mh

Electricity and Safety

A few words about working with electricity:

❖ Before attempting any repairs, make sure the power is disconnected.

❖ Never substitute electrical components without a professional inspection. If changing a fuse size, replacing breakers or a wire size, make sure a professional electrician checks out the final project.

❖ Never bypass a circuit protection device.

❖ Never work on an electrical system before you know where the power source is located.

❖ Never probe with a test light or a multimeter without knowing the kind of voltage used here.

❖ Excessive heat is the number one killer of power. Brown-outs (very low power) contribute the most to equipment damage as they force the equipment to work beyond their safety margin.

Test Equipment to Have On Hand

❖ Plug-in Meter to read voltage and polarity (See *Managing Power* for a recommendation).

❖ Test light or digital meter for 12 volt systems.

❖ Multimeter, analog or digital, for testing continuity and resistance.

Adding regular care and maintenance to your schedule can produce many carefree years with your motorhome.

Some of the topics covered in *Motorhome Care & Maintenance*:

Pre-Purchase Checkout

Maintaining the "Look"

Dealing with the Repair Shop

Air Conditioner, Refrigerator, Hot Water Heater

Batteries, Inverter, Basic Solar Technology

Sewer System

Water Pump, Filtering Your Water

Furnace

Hydraulic Leveling System

Self-Maintenance

The best care and maintenance is performed by you. Most of us do not carry out the annual service on our rigs, a job for the nearest competent service bay. We do learn to recognize the maintenance issues and prepare for them. This is the "care" in care and maintenance.

Not only cost effective, understanding how your motorhome works gives you a sense of control over this huge machine and its components.

Set Up a Maintenance Calendar

Do this on your computer with a follow-up reminder, or on a wall calendar. In *Microsoft Outlook,* the *Task* feature works well as a reminder. Several free and easy to use reminder programs are available to download from the Internet.

Keep in mind that taking care of your motorhome pays off in comfort for you and big resale value when the time comes to change lifestyles. A quality-built recreational vehicle can retain its showroom glow twenty years later if cared for in a timely manner.

❖ If desired, learn how to do the basic maintenance your-self by taking courses offered by various RV support groups and local resources

❖ Escapees RV Club has quarterly events that offer maintenance seminars

❖ Create checklists for the generator, battery, air condi-tioner, storage tanks, water heater, leveler maintenance, and annual service

❖ Read the manufacturer's manuals provided with your rig, and secure necessary manuals from other sources

❖ Carry spare parts for on-the-spot repairs

❖ If you have a wood interior, be prepared to keep condi-tioning agents on-board

Pre- Purchase Checkout

Before you purchase a motorhome, **always**, **always**, **always** have an independent RV mechanic check out the vehicle before you sign on the dotted line. This process can save headaches and money later.

Minimum pre-purchase examination checklist:

- Air Conditioners (roof and engine-driven)
- Awning
- Batteries (test for life cycle)
- Door lock
- Engine
- Hydraulic levelers
- Propane system (test for leaks)
- Roof coating and seals around vents, air conditioner, and antennas
- Slideout seals (if applicable)
- Refrigerator
- Water Heater
- Window seals

Things you can check yourself:

- Microwave
- Window shades/blinds and light fixtures
- Water flow
- Toilet

Often RV repair shops offer a free checkout service, hoping to charge the owner to fix the items that wind up on the checklist. Other mobile service people might charge $100 to spend the hour necessary. Depending on the results, you may be able to negotiate a drop in the asking price.

If you purchase through an RV dealer (not recommended), hire a certified RV Inspector come to the lot (NRVIA.com to find one in your area). Always make arrangements to be present during the inspection.

Do not skip this step no matter what tale the sales person spins. If they refuse to cooperate, walk away. Something is wrong with the motorhome, regardless of the exterior/interior appearance or change in price.

The point being that most people trade in RVs when they begin to suspect expensive repair bills are coming soon.

Most RV dealers take vehicles in trade without regard to condition. The dealer's profit margin is so high on the newer model just sold this customer, they can afford to do this. If the exterior is presentable, some unsuspecting newbie drives it off the lot.

This is similar to the way people value their automobiles. If they enjoy a vehicle, they continue to keep up the maintenance until it overwhelms them with repair costs. If it is junk to start with, they get rid of it sooner.

On the other hand, some people sell their RV because they want a new feature, a new layout, a diesel rather than a gas engine. Some sell because of ill health or lifestyle change. If possible, buy your first RV from an owner in this category.

Maintaining the "Look"

Once you find the perfect motorhome, enjoy keeping the exterior paint fresh and glossy. It is pleasing to the eye and ups the resale value enormously.

Preventing roof runoff, those black streaks, from fouling up the sidewall paint may not be possible, but you can keep these streaks from embedding into the exterior paint by waxing often. The new spray "auto detail" waxes available now do an excellent job. They are easy to apply, spray on and wipe off the excess.

If the body sidewalls are fiberglass, not aluminum, upkeep is not as easy. It requires a liquid wax, such as Nu Finish, to add shine.

While you are sitting outside enjoying the view, keep an eye on the exterior condition of the RV. Not allowing dirt and stains to accumulate on the paint job keeps your RV looking almost showroom perfect.

Depending on the size of your RV, a complete wash and wax job can be exhausting. However, spending an hour a week touching up with a spray wax makes all the difference in the "look."

Installing the proper side gutters on your motorhome, to direct the runoff from the air conditioner and rainfall, could prove worth the money, since gutters save time keeping the "look" alive.

Dealing with the Repair Shop

With all the horror stories floating around about the RV repair business, who can you trust to take care of major repairs or install add-ons to personalize your RV.

❖ Ask at the RV park front desk for reliable services that guests recommended.

❖ Always ask for a written work order with the repairs or services written down and a cost estimate explained in detail. Request that they place *right on the work order* that any extra costs over $100 requires a phone call and approval from you **before** any work is performed. *Make sure that you walk away with a copy of the work order.*

❖ Do not hesitate to discuss the final bill with the shop owner if you have a problem with it.

❖ If the shop refuses to follow your guidelines, find another vendor in the area.

❖ Woodworking and cabinet making is the most expensive and frustrating project of them all. Finding a quality craftsman that can fulfill your dream is difficult. Keep looking until you get a referral from someone that has personal experience with the artisan.

If possible, look at a finished project to see if it meets your expectations. After finding the right artist, expect to spend several weeks waiting for the end result.

❖ A word to the wise: Before making any expensive cosmetic changes, make sure you are happy enough with your first RV to keep it for a few years. Any upgrades you make now are most likely not going to render any monetary gain when you sell it. Try to hold down the tendency to re-decorate until you live in it for at least six months.

Windshield Wipers

Ron McNevin shared this great tip in Motorhome Magazine.

"Windshield wiper blades can be quite expensive to replace. I discovered a cheap way to provide UV protection.

I bought 3/8- to 1/2-inch foam pipe insulation, cut it in half and wrapped it around the blades. Now I have protection for the wipers and it cost me less than $2."

Great idea, Ron, one I share myself. When on the road, in dry weather, you can even drive with them installed.

Awning

Taking care of the patio and window awnings is one of those tasks that is essential. Two types of material are used in your average awning construction, acrylic and vinyl.

Each awning material has its own specifications for maintenance. Vinyl is the easiest to care for as soap and water works fine.

The material does not endure as long, nor does it have the colorful, rich look of the acrylic fabric.

Mildew does not form on the awning material itself, but on the dust and debris it collects. Keep the awning clean with soap and water.

Since acrylic is not waterproof, caring for this awning fabric requires a non-soap detergent, such as *Woolite*. This prevents opening the weave of the fabric and allowing moisture to leak. There are specialty cleaners available too.

Maintenance Guide

❖ When opening the awning for the first time, note the condition of the awning arms, roller, and the fabric.

❖ Each time you open the awning, take note of the condition. Catching little signs of damage can prevent having to replace the fabric.

❖ Keep the fabric from stretching during the rainy season by lowering one arm of the awning. This allows the rain to drain off rather than pool in the middle. If the awning starts to sag with the water overload, it causes the roller to bend. The awning then becomes a problem that can only be solved by replacing parts or the complete awning itself.

❖ Keep an eye on the weather and always roll the awning up when high winds are predicted. Updrafts can tear the awning off the vehicle.

❖ When traveling, secure the arms with Velcro straps that keep the material from unfurling in high winds. Pay a little extra to make sure that your awning has an aluminum or vinyl shield. If no shield is attached, a strap for the middle of the awning is always a good idea.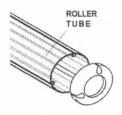

ROLLER TUBE

❖ When at the campsite, use a set of "de-flappers" attached to the loose part of the awning. This stretches the center part of the fabric and prevents it from flapping in the wind.

❖ Apply Silicone lubricant to the threaded shafts of all locking knobs to resist corrosion.

❖ Use a spray silicone lubricant on all sliding parts of the awning hardware.

❖ Check all arm pivot points for enlargement of holes or broken rivets.

❖ Check the awning for loose stitching and possible shrinkage or puckering of the fabric.

❖ When closing the awning, ensure that the awning strap is evenly distributed along the roller.

NOTES:

Roof Maintenance

At least twice a year, clean the RV roof with detergent and water. Sometimes the entire roof is black caused by dirt, debris, and composted leaves. Scrub using a stiff brush and rinse thoroughly.

If you have aluminum or fiberglass siding on your RV, the popping sound you hear from time to time is the chassis structure flexing. Caused from temperature change and simply traveling down the road, this flexing requires that the roof covering be flexible too. Aging and lack of maintenance can create a costly roof replacement.

Keep a close watch on the condition of the roof. Even rubber and PermaSeal roofs need attention. Leaks are the greatest cause of wood rot and structure failure, not to mention ugly discoloration of the interior headliner.

❖ Check for cracks caused by sunlight exposure and the normal flexing of the chassis

❖ Check around all the vents, skylights and air conditioner for cracks

❖ The biggest hazard is where the fiberglass caps attach to the front and rear of the roof. When those cap seals crack, often at the corners (from vibration, heat, and cold stress and age), water leaks down into the interior

Repairing the Roof

A few products used to seal the roof are mentioned here. Before using any of these products, all previous sealants, tapes, and patches must be removed. All caulking needs to be removed. The roof must be washed and scrubbed clean with a firm bristle brush to remove all residue. Some products need a primer.

Suggestion: If doing the repair job yourself, for small leaks that are not in the cap seams, start with the *EternaBond Doublestick* tape.

> ➤ First, find where the water is leaking into the interior (see *How To Find The Source of a Link*)

> ➤ Spend the time to clean the area first with a stiff brush and rinse, or the tape does not seal

If you buy a used motorhome and find the roof is leaking, consider spending the money to have a professional roof coating applied before wood rot creates a whole new problem. This ensures the end of leaks. Patching with a Dicor sealant or EternaBond tape is a short-term approach.

Types of Roof Repair

PermaSeal: an elastic polyurethane coating that resembles rubber. It is sprayed over any roof surface. Spraying right up to the edge of vents, skylights and over the cap seams on each end of the roof, eliminates any possibility of leaks. Impervious to humidity, mold and fungus, this coating has a long life. Leaks are a thing of the past with reasonable care taken not to slice or cut this thick covering.

When sprayed on it dries within 15 minutes. PermaSeal is available in 24-oz. aerosol cans, gallons or sprayed over the entire roof. This coating can be painted when dry. If applied by professionals, the warranty is 10 years before recoating is required.

RoofMate: an elastomeric Acrylic roof coating with high tensile strength. Non-Flammable. Easy, roll-on application. Quick curing. Suitable for about 6 years before recoat. Prime before using.

Ultra Shield: An elastomeric acrylic roof coating. Easy to apply (roll-on). Quick cure. Non-flammable. Comes in several standard colors. Suitable for about 5 years before recoat. Prime before using.

Dicor Elastomeric Metal RV Roof Coating: A similar elastomeric coating but is not recommended for rubber or TPO (Thermoplastic polyolefin) roof repairs. Two coats required with a 24-hour cure period.

EternaBond Doublestick tape: Used for small roof repairs. This tape does not work well on the cap seams and cannot be used over silicone products.

Dicor Ultra Sealant: A high performance adhesive/sealant providing excellent, long lasting superior adhesion and durability. Similar in appearance to caulking, it is applied the same way with a caulking gun. This sealant can be used for TPO roofing.

Often mobile repair businesses use this to stop leaks as it is inexpensive and quick to apply. It must be applied smoothly and not in goopy chunks (shown below) that crack with temperature changes, breaking the seal.

Not a good application of sealant.

Replacing the Roof Coating

The only problem found when doing the pre-purchase check on my current used motorhome was the roof and some fiberglass damage in the rear. The owner promised to fix the roof and discounted the purchase price for the exterior damage to be repaired later.

As it turned out, he used EternaBond on the cap seams that, of course, did not hold. I spent several hundred dollars on Dicor sealant repair jobs, but nothing worked.

Finally, I spent the money to get a PermaSeal roof (longest warranty). Problem now solved for at least 10 years. After spraying on the basic black coating, they run the coating (by hand brush) right up to the vents and skylight edges, sealing off any possible leaks. A white reflective paint is rolled on.

How To Find The Source Of A Leak

According to Curtis Carter at *FunTimesGuide.com*:

"The first step should be a good water test--one that takes some time--as you may need to allow the water to travel its path before you see it coming into the interior space. I recommend using a garden hose with the nozzle set on a wide spray.

Take your time, with one person on the inside watching and another working their way spraying water along all seams, roof vents, and even the side wall itself.

Do not forget any windows that may be involved. The air conditioner on the roof is sealed with a foam rubber gasket placed underneath the unit. Be sure to run water around that gasket as it can migrate to other spots.

Start your water test from the ground up, as soon as water shows up inside, problem solved. That way, you know for sure if the leak is in the vertical seam or somewhere else."

Moisture Meter

One tool I found to be helpful is a reliable moisture meter. This is one way to find out if water is pooling somewhere out of sight. The General MMD4E Moisture Meter is my choice. If you find wood rot, it needs to be fixed before recoating the roof.

Available at Amazon.com

NOTES:

Air Conditioner

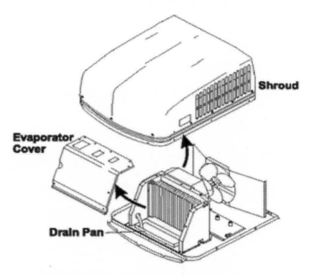

A roof mounted RV air conditioner operates only on 120 V power. It requires a generator capable of providing 2800 watts, or more.

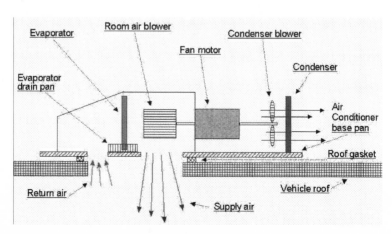

Maintenance Procedures

➤ Check and clean the inside filter frequently.

➤ Visually check the roof gasket at least once a year. The gasket should $\frac{1}{2}$ -inch thick.

➤ Roof bolts should be checked and tightened, if necessary, at least once a year.

➤ Check the drain holes at least once a year.

➤ Clean the dirt and debris from the evaporator coils at least once a year.

➤ Inspect the rear fins on the back of the unit to make sure that they are not crushed.

Managing Power, AC and DC

Vital components inside any RV manufactured after 1980, specifically those run by electronics, are exposed to sudden termination by a low-power situation. RV parks of all types, whether commercial or private resort, have problems, from time to time, delivering 120 volts to your rig. This is known in the RV community as "brownouts."

Line Monitor

Buy an AC *line monitor* with a digital readout that plugs into an AC outlet. Keep your eye on this meter to gauge the voltage available for use. Pay particular attention to this reading before turning on the microwave or air conditioning.

Power Manager

Solve the low-power problem you find in older RV parks by purchasing a *Hughes Autoformer* power manager.

These are very expensive ($350-$650) but worth the investment if you live full-time or spend a season in your motorhome. Most of the electrical problems like surges, spikes and brown-outs are handled by this power manager.

This heavy weather-resistant metal box is designed to protect your motorhome equipment from damage caused by low power called "brownouts" (see below).

Not just a power transformer, these units are designed to take any voltage spike and protect power systems.

If the spike is powerful enough, these units burn out instead of the microwave, air conditioner, or other appliance. The manufacturer has a return plan in place should that burnout event occur.

From the *Autoformer* manufacturer's website:

"The unit does not take power from the park. It does not affect the park or input voltage, or make electricity.

What it is doing is changing the voltage-amperage relationship, lowering the amperage and raising the voltage. Since appliances run better on higher voltage, lower amperage, less overall power is used from the park, and better service is enjoyed from your RV.

A unit running at full output (50 Amps) uses 1 Amp, but causes appliances to cycle more often and run cooler. This uses less total power from the park.

- ❖ 30 and 50 Amp models are available.
- ❖ As demand changes, the output is adjusted.
- ❖ Run air conditioning and more of your appliances at the same time."

Get more information and dealer locations from the manufacturer: www.**HughesAutoformer.com**.

[Also available at *Amazon.com* with free shipping.]

Electrical System Protection

If you choose not to install an Autoformer, protection needs to be installed to protect your valuable appliances, TV, Stereo and computers.

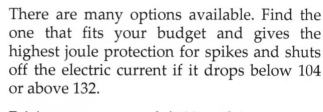

There are many options available. Find the one that fits your budget and gives the highest joule protection for spikes and shuts off the electric current if it drops below 104 or above 132.

Pricing starts around $100 and increases to $350 for the full range protection. Unlike the Autoformer, no voltage boosting is available with these units.

Circuit Breakers and Fuse Boxes

One of the first things on your motorhome checklist is to find and label the circuit breakers and fuse boxes. They may be in separate locations or right next to each other.

Match each breaker to the location of the interior electric outlets so you know which breaker to move to the OFF position in a stress-related situation.

Remember, always disconnect the power before changing fuses. It is wise to carry extra fuses, but circuit breaker replacements need to be done by an electrician.

Find the GFCI (Ground Fault Circuit Interrupter) circuits inside and possibly one in the outside power cabinet, and label them. This is the first thing to check when the power to only one of the circuits in your motorhome shuts down. This may affect only one or two electrical outlets.

The kitchen and bathroom may have a GFCI. Check the outside power cabinet where your inverter is connected.

There is a little button on the receptacle that clicks off to protect the circuit. Once you have located and corrected the reason for the shutoff, push the button in for a few seconds to re-start the power to this circuit.

Approximately AMP Ratings

120 VAC

Appliance	Amps
Air conditioner	13
Coffee maker	12
Water heater (electric)	12
Washer/dryer	13
Microwave	8
Convection	15
Refrigerator	3.5
Converter (charging)	8
Space heater (1600 watts)	13
Space heater (800 watts)	6.5
Iron	8
Electric blanket	2
Hair dryer (1500 watts)	13
Hair dryer (400 watts)	3.5
Curling iron	0.7
TV	.5-1.0
VCR	0.2
Computer	2

12 VDC

Appliance or Accessory	Estimated AMPs
Aisle Light	1
CO Detector	1
Fluorescent Light	1-2
Furnace	10-12
LP Gas Leak Detector	1
Overhead lights (Per Bulb)	1
Porch Light	1
Power Roof Vent	1.5
Radio/Stereo	4
Range Hood (Fan & Light	2-3
Refrigerator (LP Gas Mode)	1.5- 2
Security System	1
Television (12 volt)	4-5
TV Antenna Booster	<1
TV Antenna Booster 12 Volt outlet	Up to 8
Variable Speed Ceiling / Vent Fan	4
VCR Recorder / Player	2
Water Pump	4

Electric Cable Adapter for External Use

Motorhomes are designed either to run on a 30-Amp or a 50-Amp electrical connection. In one of the storage compartments outside is the *electrical bay*.

Inside is a long, thick cable wired into the motorhome that provides all AC electrical connections on the inside. This cable is plugged into the AC power pedestal provided by the RV park.

> **Note**: that a 50-Amp cable is very thick and heavy to lug around. Its plug has **three prongs** and a rounded ground prong.
>
> A 30-Amp cable is much thinner and lighter with **two prongs** and a rounded ground prong.

For a more technical explanation, visit this link:
rvbasics.com/techtips/50-to-30-Amp-adapter.html

This AC connection to the park power pedestal provides current to the air conditioner, microwave, all electrical outlets, and some overhead interior lights.

All but very old RV parks provide 30-Amp service on the AC power pedestal somewhere on the site. 50-Amp service is a relatively new upgrade for most parks and an extra service charge usually applies.

Some of the newer parks offer only 50-Amp service. Others offer 30-Amp and 50-Amp service from the same post.

If the motorhome comes equipped with 50-Amp service, then a 50- to 30-Amp adapter should be a part of your electrical accessories since most overnight stays between destinations may be in older parks.

Purchase an adapter that has a small length of cable between each end for ease of use. Plug the female end to your RV electrical cable, the male end to the power pedestal in the park.

Amperage Adapters

30- to 50-Amp

If your motorhome runs on 30-Amp, use a 30-to-50 Amp adapter to be able to hook up to a 50-Amp power pedestal. Simply plug in the female end of the adapter to your motorhome electrical cable and the male end to the 50-Amp power pedestal on your site.

This **does not** give the motorhome 50-Amp service, but it does improve the quality of the voltage used.

50-to-30-Amp

If your motorhome runs on 50-Amp, use a 50-to-30 Amp adapter to be able to hook up to a 30-Amp power pedestal. Simply plug in the female end of the adapter to your motorhome electrical cable  and the male end to the 30-Amp power pedestal on your site. Keep your eye on the inside digital voltage meter, as the motorhome is now running on 30-Amp power.

Batteries

Many of the systems in a motorhome interact and one system can affect the performance of another. There are two different types of battery systems in any Class A or Class C.

Engine Battery

Some motorhome manufacturers use the engine battery to power the radio and cockpit cigarette lighter sockets, other manufacturers use the coach battery system for these features. Check the coach documentation to find out how your coach distributes this power system. It is important to keep this battery charged properly.

The engine battery is usually located near the generator or tucked in underneath the front hood like a car battery. A sealed battery works fine as it gets little use.

Coach Batteries

Coach batteries are a different system that provides DC (not AC) electricity to the interior of the coach, for example, the overhead vent fans and most of the interior lighting. If disconnected from any outside electrical source, these batteries give all the current to the coach (see *Inverter*).

Coach batteries are often located under the entrance steps or nearby outside compartment. These batteries are constantly being discharged by any interior demand requiring DC voltage.

An ongoing debate exists about the best type of RV coach battery to buy: Flooded acid (wet cells), gelled acid (gel cells) or AGM (absorbed glass mat).

The latest upgrade in coach batteries being tested for RV use is Lithium-Ion. It is an exciting dream to be able to carry all the power you need, indefinitely.

Visit **www.technomadia.com/lithium** for details.

The quick answer is two deep-cycle 12 V flooded acid batteries. *Interstate* is the brand most commonly available (Sears, Wal-Mart) and reasonably priced.

Storage space dictates the actual number of batteries. If parking off the electrical grid appeals to you (boondocking), find more storage space in nearby cabinets.

Almost all batteries supplied with new motorhomes are flooded acid batteries. If you purchase a high-end motorhome, it may have one of the other battery types.

Flooded acid batteries are the most common lead acid battery because they are cheaper and lighter in weight. Small motorhomes (25-30 feet) work perfectly fine on flooded acid batteries. *My flooded acid batteries need replacing every three years, so be prepared rather than surprised.*

➢ Estimate the amount of boondocking (no outside power source) on your itinerary and whether solar panels are installed on the roof.

➢ Check to see how much room is available in the outside basement or under the entrance steps in the motorhome to store and hook up these batteries, in case you want more.

➢ Replacing a group 24 battery with a group 27 or even a group 29, physically larger and heavier, provides more power over a longer period of time.

Tip: *Check the top of your coach battery for a "group" number.*

Overcharging and undercharging are the main reasons batteries deteriorate, but not keeping the water level constant is also a contributing factor. Having an *Inverter* wired into the system eliminates the charging issues, but you control the water level.

Before deciding how many batteries are required, keep in mind that the microwave/convection oven and the toaster oven do not generally operate without a good park electrical power source or a generator. It takes 2800 watts of capacity to run the average microwave. Ergo, there is no point to four batteries if two is all you need.

Here is a website link that provides detailed information to help you make a choice.

www.interstatebatteries.com/m/category/rv

Battery Maintenance

If your batteries are new, on your calendar, every 3 months, mark down "check battery water." If they are several years old, check every month. Remember our motto, "take care of your vehicle, and it takes care of you," well, this is certainly true for batteries.

Always use *Distilled Water* to replace the fluid inside the cells. I use a large eyedropper for control to make sure that no overfilling occurs. Enough air space must remain so expansion can take place.

The red circles on the battery top (see below) mark the cell covers. Gently pry them up with a non-metallic tool. Fill the cells to ⅛" below the fill well. Make sure the cover is re-seated firmly; I usually tap the cover a few times.

Do Not Overfill!

If your batteries do not have removable cell covers, they are sealed batteries and no maintenance is required.

Good safety rules dictate that proper clothing, gloves and safety glasses be worn when handling batteries.

In a new fully charged battery (less than a year old), no more than a few large eye droppers full of water is usually needed for each cell. Sometimes no water is required. Add water to 1/8" below the bottom of the fill well.

If you find cells that require a lot of water, it is possible that the battery needs to be replaced soon. In the meantime, change the calendar reminder to every two weeks. You do not want the battery to boil over and become a possible fire hazard.

If the battery is discharged, add water to a level **just above** the plates, allowing for expansion while charging.

To clean acid residue on the terminals, batteries, or the battery bracket, use a solution of baking soda and water. Purchase a special corrosion-protection spray for the terminals, available at any auto store (and on Amazon).

When changing batteries, best practice is to clean the battery bracket before inserting the new batteries. The acid residue continues to eat away at the metal bracket if not removed. Use baking soda and water to clean the bracket.

Ensure that the terminals are properly tightened; terminals that are too tight or too loose could result in post breakage, meltdown or fire.

Important: Some batteries, when the cells run dry, are a fire hazard. Keep flames, sparks or metal objects away from battery location.

Solar Panel for Battery Charging

To keep a balanced charge to your engine and/or house batteries, adding a small solar panel may be the solution.

For detailed information, visit

www.outsidesupply.com/rv-solar-guide/

The Basics of Solar Technology

Solar is a costly addition but may repay the investment in one year if it enables you to boondock often. With commercial park rates soaring higher every year, the $500 to $3,000+ cost for parts and installation may prove to be a good investment.

Enjoying the beauty and solitude that nature offers, versus sitting in a paved parking lot, may be incentive enough to justify the cost of the panels and controller.

Solar panels (or modules) fall into three types, single crystal, multicrystalline, and amorphous. These references are to the type of surface that is sandwiched between, usually glass, and a type of thin encapsulation on the back.

❖ The single crystal solar panel is known to be the oldest and most efficient of the solar technologies. It translates approximately 15 to 18% of the sun's light into electricity.

❖ The multicrystalline or polycrystalline panels uses chips sliced from single crystals. Multicrystalline panels translate approximately 14% of the sun's light into electricity.

❖ The amorphous panels are made by sending an aluminum substrate through a vacuum chamber where the silicon gas is blown on top. Amorphous panels are the least efficient at 6-8%.

❖ You can identify most single crystal panels by their solid one-color solar cells, the multicrystalline by their cells that are chip-like, and the amorphous, usually brown and one complete surface.

Single Crystalline: For a motorhome where space is at a premium, the single crystalline can deliver the most power in the smallest size.

Multicrystalline: Not as small as the single crystalline but close, and has the advantage of being less expensive.

Amorphous: This panel can take up double the space of a single crystalline.

The amount of charging power a solar panel puts out is directly proportional to the intensity of the sunlight.

> ➤ Decrease the level of sunlight to half that of a bright sunny day and the charging power is reduced by half.

> ➤ Park your motorhome in a dusty parking lot for a few days and the panel output reduces.

> ➤ Heat also negatively affects the output of solar electric panels.

> ➤ Contrary to the general public's perception, solar electric panels are run off of the sun's light not heat. In fact, the hotter the panel, or more exact the cell gets, the less efficient.

> ➤ The best place for solar electricity is up in space or in the high mountains where it is clean, clear and cold.

Rating Solar Panels

All solar panels have a detailed energy label on the back. Find the watts, volts and amps.

For the layperson, the three pieces of information to pull out are the **watts, volts,** and **amps**. In "solar speak" they are known as:

> ❖ **Watts**: Nominal Peak Power (P max)
> ❖ **Voltage**: Peak Power Voltage (Vmp)
> ❖ **Amps**: Peak Power Current (Imp).

These are the conditions the solar panel can experience when hooked up to the battery.

Quality of Solar Panels

Most solar panels come with 10-20 year warranties. It is extremely difficult to break a solar panel even though most are covered in glass. Extreme testing is required before getting to market.

Basic Requirements for Panels

❖ Look for panels that are 17 volts or higher. This voltage allows for enough voltage drop to be able to charge the batteries to the target of 14.2 volts.

❖ A 17-volt panel can be identified by looking at the front of the solar panel and being able to count 36 cells. As each cell is just under one-half of a volt and these are tied together, a **36 cell panel** generally means at least 17 volts.

❖ A **30 or 33 cell panel** does not belong on the roof of a motorhome for true solar charging.

Controllers

Charge controllers sit between the solar panel and the batteries. They are also called regulators. Regulator is a bit more clear because their job is to regulate the flow of the electricity from the solar panels to the batteries so that the solar panels do not overcharge the batteries. A few examples are shown here.

❖ They protect the batteries from being overcharged by regulating the solar energy.

❖ Most have a blocking diode or one-way gate that does not allow your battery energy to flow out through the solar panel at night.

❖ Many have meters that show the amps coming from the solar panel and the voltage of the battery.

❖ Some have just an LED that shows that the panel is charging and flashes when the battery is fully charged.

Basic Regulating Technologies

Shunt Modulation

Shunt technology has been around for quite a while. Electronic circuitry measures the battery voltage.

As voltage increases to a preset number, the solar energy is switched off or diverted, stopping dead the flow of solar energy to the battery. At some resumption set point, charging resumes.

❖ The draw back with the shunt controller is that it is either on or off.

❖ When the preset reconnect voltage is attained, it dumps all the available energy from the solar into the battery.

This can boil water out of your batteries. While this type of controller is a low cost option, newer technologies have been proven to be nicer to your batteries.

Pulse Width Modulation

Pulse Width Modulation (PWM) is now very standard as the best you can get at an affordable price. PWM has been proven to keep your batteries at the highest state of charge, and uses the least amount of water consumption.

❖ Initially during the day, all the solar energy goes directly to the battery. Immediately after a preset voltage is reached, a PWM Taper Charge begins, and the preset battery voltage is maintained by switching the solar energy source on/off.

❖ After the preset voltage is reached and stabilized by the PWM, a float (trickle) charge is effected to hold the battery at the preset voltage.

Temperature Compensation

Temperature compensation is achieved by running a wire from the controller to the batteries. At the end of the temperature compensation line is a probe that reacts to the temperature; this reaction is then sensed by the controller to change the solar charging voltage.

Inverter

Inverters are electronic devices that convert battery power into a form that mimics conventional grid power. Most models produce a "modified square wave."

Premium inverters produce a "pure sine wave" to imitate grid power. This eliminates background noise so that all appliances, including electronics, work without problems.

Particularly suited for sensitive electronics found in desktop computers and high-quality sound equipment, this pure sine wave inverter is expensive. Modified wave is the most common inverter installed.

The inverter in your motorhome does three jobs:

❖ Converts the battery power (DC) to AC when not plugged into an outside power source

❖ Directs DC power to the coach

❖ Charges the batteries in three or more stages, no over-charge or undercharge

All newer Class A coaches should come equipped with an inverter/charger. Check this before purchasing any motorhome, particularly a Class C.

To add an inverter is an expensive project. Even with a small solar panel, the 1000-Watt size inverter is the best choice for a motorhome under 30 feet.

Keep in mind that the microwave/convection oven and toaster oven generally do not run on battery power only, so when boondocking these appliances are not available. It takes 2500 watts to run those energy-hungry appliances and requires a pure sine inverter to run them efficiently.

There are two ways to run the inverter:

- ❖ Leave the inverter on all the time and use it as a power backup when electrical glitches in the RV park system cause a brief shutdown.
- ❖ *Important*: It also keeps the batteries charged at the proper rate, no overcharge or undercharge.
- ❖ Turn it on only when boondocking. Running the engine or generator works as a charger through the inverter.

Converter

If your motorhome does not have an inverter installed, then it has a *converter*. The *converter*'s job, just the opposite of the inverter, is to change 120 volts AC to 12 volt DC to supply power to all the 12-volt appliances and accessories in the motorhome.

If you are not plugged into an outside electrical source, your coach batteries take over this job and provide 12-volt DC to the coach.

The converter's built-in battery charger is designed to keep the house batteries topped off with a trickle charge.

Older motorhome converters charge at a fixed voltage in the range of 13.5 volts. This causes the boiling over problems that diminish the life of the batteries. One of the first things to find out: Does this new-to-you rig have a three-stage charger in the converter?

A three-stage charger/converter should be installed that can provide a bulk charge then an absorption charge and finally a float charge. Newer RV converters on the market are capable of charging the batteries this way.

If your batteries are fully charged, this can be too much for a float charge and over time it depletes the water level in the batteries cells. This is why it is important to check the water level in your batteries on a regular basis.

The 45W converter/charger pictured here has a 3-phase charger at about half the price of an inverter. If you stay connected to park power all the time and no sensitive computer equipment to worry about, this looks like a good buy.

Find the documentation on your charger (try an online search) and determine if it has the new 3-stage charger. If it is not equipped with a staged charger, keep a close eye on the water level in the batteries.

The charger could be located near the electric cable in an outside cabinet.

Generator

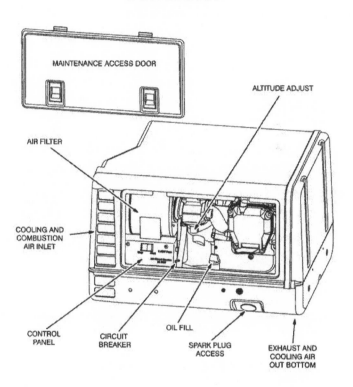

A generator supplies the coach with electricity to run all the lights and appliances, just as though you are connected to an outside electric source. It draws its fuel from the gas or diesel tank that supplies the engine, or a larger propane tank is provided for this purpose.

Before you leave on your first trip, have the generator serviced by an RV mechanic that *specializes in generator maintenance*. The oil/filter may need to be changed and the spark plugs checked.

Important: Before turning OFF the generator, ensure that the air conditioner is already OFF. The same applies when you turn the generator ON.

This sudden shift in voltage sucks oil into the combustion chamber of the generator and fouls the plugs.

Maintenance Procedures

When not using the generator, regular maintenance is required. To keep it running smoothly, ensure that it runs *no less than 30 minutes once every three months*. Mark your calendar. This routine works well for my 4000 Onan.

Running the generator during a *rest stop* along your travel path is a good way to handle this maintenance chore.

This maintenance must be continued even if you store your motorhome more than three months. Adding a fuel conditioner to the gas/diesel tank may help to extend the maintenance beyond the three-month requirement.

What happens if you do not keep up the maintenance? The generator stops working just when you need it the most. A costly repair replacing the carburetor may also ensue.

 ➤ Every 50 hours, change the oil and filter. It takes about 3 quarts of oil. Change the spark plugs too as part of the maintenance procedure.

 ➤ If spending time near ocean areas where salt water creates corrosion, do the maintenance procedure more often.

Generators are designed to last for a long time when properly maintained. Download the free *"Onan Gas Genset Maintenance Schedule"* from my webpage:

TheRVLifestyle.MovingOnWithMargo.com#mh.

Sewer System

Sewer Hose

If you buy a used motorhome, it already has several sewer hoses and connectors. You may find that they have reached their end-of-life. When purchasing new sewer hoses, buy the *Valterra Viper* kit (or something similar) and another 5- and/or 10-foot extension of the same brand.

Parking Site Sewer End

RV End

The Viper hose is made of tougher and more flexible material than the cheaper variety. It has a built-in adapter for the motorhome connection and a seal for the park sewer connection, a clean and neat solution.

Add the extension when the sewer connection is more than 15 feet from your motorhome. There are also times when the park sewer opening is less than ten feet from the motorhome connection.

This is the time to use the extension after adding the park sewer end from the original 15-foot hose. Buying the same brand for both hoses is essential for an easy switch out.

There are less expensive kits but be prepared to fix or discard these hoses after a few months. Because this lower quality hose is rigid and can collapse into itself (making it easy to store), the hose ridges split from the slightest pressure allowing black water to spill onto the ground.

This is a big no-no with state health departments and strictly enforced.

When buying the new sewer hose kit, also pick up what is called a "sewer donut." This donut is not used in most states, but once in a while a certain county regulation requires it.

These are inexpensive and look like rubber donuts with one side elongated and narrower than the other side. Squeeze it into any park sewer receptacle and make a generic fit for any sewer hose fitting. Some parks do not allow you to hook up without one.

Tips For A Happy Toilet

For the best smelling results (none) in the bathroom, keep it simple: Do not flush toilet paper.

Store the toilet paper in a lidded container nearby. This keeps paper from fouling the sensors in the black water tank or creating a blockage that is hard to clear. Paper also creates its own smell that takes a long time to break down in the tank.

Tip: During hot summer days, add an ounce of *Happy Camper Organic Holding Tank Treatment* to the toilet tank. Order it online or from a local RV supply store. It stops the odor instantly. Otherwise, use inexpensive non-scented laundry detergent (more on this later).

Emptying the Gray and Black Water Tanks

1. Remove the protective cap that covers the sewer connection. Attach the sewer hose as indicated in the picture below. Test the hose to make sure the connector is securely fastened to the corresponding notches.

2. **Slowly open ONLY the black water tank valve an inch or so.** Check for leaks at the connection point, if none, open the tank valve all the way. Wait a few moments to make sure the tank is empty, then **close the valve**.

3. Pull and leave the gray water valve open. This rinses the black water from the hose and avoids a mess when storing the hose.

4. Leave the gray water valve open until just before the next black water dump. This eliminates the need for frequent dumps of the gray water tank to keep it from overflowing into the shower/tub.

3. Pull Grey Water Valve Leave Open Until Just Before Time to Dump Black Water Again | GREY WATER | BLACK WATER | 2. Pull Black Water Valve Empty Tank then Close

1. Remove CAP
SEWER CONNECTION
Attach Sewer Connection

Important: Replace the cap when traveling to your next destination. Some states may cite you for traveling down the road with liquid dripping from the sewer pipe.

Routine Tank-dumping Procedure

1. After the tank is clean, pour one capful of laundry detergent (scent-free) into the toilet. Allow a little water to flow in with the detergent. From now on, follow this procedure after every dump.

2. Leave the outside **gray water** tank valve **open** until you see on the inside gauge (or smell) the need to drain the black water tank. This eliminates dumping the gray water frequently to prevent backups into the shower. Mark the calendar for the next dump date.

Important: Always keep the outside **black water** tank valve **closed** between dumps. Liquid needs to build up to keep the contents from forming hard clumps.

If you smell blowback from the tank, check the outside valve for a leak. Valve replacement may be necessary, Replace the valve yourself, or hire a mobile vendor.

3. Close the outside gray water valve a couple of days before the black water tank is full. Take a few showers or wash several batches of dishes.

4. On moving day, remember to add one capful of scent-free laundry detergent to the toilet before pulling the outside black water valve.

Note: The electronic sensor lights on the inside control panel are not reliable in older motorhomes, so only use them as a heads-up and mark the calendar.

If the motorhome is 5 years old or newer, add a capful of liquid (or powder) Calgon Water Softener (WalMart carries this) to the tank along with the laundry detergent.

This keeps the sensors free of water deposits and improves sensor accuracy. Older motorhome tank sensors (depending on the amount of prior maintenance) may not be restored to accuracy by any method.

> **Caution**: Do not forget that the gray water valve is closed prior to the dump cycle. When you see the shower/tub fill with gray water from below, it is past time to empty the tanks.

> **Important**: Never leave the motorhome unattended for any length of time *with the gray water valve closed*. If a Reverse Osmosis water filter system is installed, it adds water to the gray water tank until the pressurized water storage tank is full. This can add ten gallons or more to the gray water tank.

Black Water Tank Maintenance

On your first outing with your motorhome, clean the black water tank using a wand inserted into the toilet from inside. You can purchase these at any RV store or WalMart.

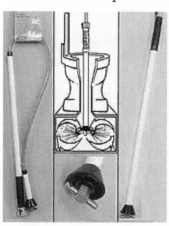

This cleaning wand is a piece of PVC pipe with a cap to keep the water from running out the end.

Two models are shown here; one has a flex wand, the other a straight wand.

Turn off the outside water. Feeding your hose through a window, attach the water hose to this wand and insert it down into the tank. Turn on the outside water and rotate the wand often. Use 5-10 minutes of high water pressure to clean the tank.

Water Bandit

To keep from dragging the hose in through a window, purchase a *Water Bandit,* a rubber attachment that fits over the bathroom faucet.

One end of the *Bandit* has a regular male hose end. Attach a short hose to the wand, turn on the water at the bathroom faucet, and you are in business. The water bandit is available at any hardware store.

As long as no toilet paper goes into the black water tank, the cleaning wand used every six months works well.

Gray Water Tank Maintenance

To keep odors out of the gray water tank, pour a cup of baking soda into the kitchen sink drain every few months.

I keep a small box of baking soda in my refrigerator to absorb odors. After a few months, I toss the baking soda down the kitchen drain (after using it to scrub the sink), followed by plenty of water.

 This is called "practical recycling."

Place a stainless steel fine mesh strainer-type cover in the sink drain opening to catch the food particles that contribute to the odor. *Happy Camper Organic Holding Tank Treatment* works well here too.

Propane Tank

Checking for propane leaks should be a top priority before purchasing a motorhome. Most RV repair services carry a simple vacuum tool that attaches to the stovetop. If a leak exists, the vacuum is broken.

When you take your motorhome out of storage, this test should be part of the pre-trip maintenance.

To turn off the propane for any reason, find the large valve handle similar to the one shown below. Turn the knob to the right just as if you were turning off water (see photo, turnoff valve inside black circle).

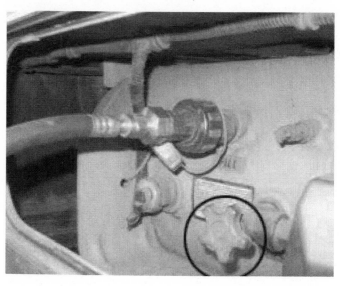

Propane does not degrade or create a hazard when sitting unused. The tank can be turned on again if necessary without calling a repairperson to make adjustments.

A distinctive odor similar to "rotten eggs" seeps into the interior of the motorhome when the propane runs low.

This odor is added intentionally (federal regulation) to warn you it is time to fill up. The smell could also be a leak warning. Propane itself has no smell.

Hot Water Heater

Unless your rig has an "instant on" hot water heater, keeping this little heater working properly can be a challenge. Propane gas is the normal fuel that feeds it, igniting through a small tube.

The design itself is part of the problem. Except for the gas instant-on product with its own drawbacks, no improvement seems imminent.

Use Electric Only or Combination

Older motorhomes sported hot water heaters fueled by propane only. The newer model motorhomes are equipped with a dual hot water heaters, propane and/or electric.

With the high price of propane, adding an electric element (Lightning Rod) to the older hot water heater may be more efficient.

It does take longer for the water to heat up when using just the electric element, but using both propane and electricity at the same time is possible too.

Nightly and weekly rates at an RV park always include the cost of electricity. Monthly stays where you pay the electric bill, the Lightning Rod element does add to the cost.

During the *pre-purchase inspection*, make sure that the propane system is checked for leaks. If this important item falls off the list, have a certified technician check it now for use later.

Most RV repair technicians have a simple vacuum tool that attaches to the stovetop propane source. If there are no breaks in the vacuum gage, no leaks.

Troubleshooting the Water Heater

What is that Noise?

When the noise is coming from the propane burner, it could be that the air-mixing gate is turned wrong. This is the where the gas enters the burner tube. *(See photo above.)*

The burner tube brings in air to stir with the propane. If it is not pulling in air properly, a noise is sometimes heard.

If not enough air is mixing with the propane, the flame is low and does not burn as hot. This can cause the water heater not to keep enough heated water in the tank.

Adjust the air intake until the noise stops.

Heater Does Not Light

The jet that the propane comes through to be lit can sometimes get clogged. Use a pipe cleaner or other tool, to clean out the jet.

If the pilot light is lit by an electronic connection, checking the wires could find a loose connection. Best practice is to call a local RV repairperson for this fix.

Check for Insect Infestation

When the water heater turns on, if you hear a loud roar and you see soot coming out of exhaust, some insect has found a new home. Open the outside door and check for nests.

Sometimes insects build nests inside the curved part of the burner tube. Clean out the burning tube with a pipe cleaner. The tube should burn clean and efficient. A faulty burn may allow carbon dioxide can leak into the interior of the coach.

Odor In The Water

If there is an odor in the water, more than likely a bacteria has built up in the heater. To remove the odor, the tank needs to be drained and flushed out with a chlorine and water mixture. This kills the bacteria. *(See Flushing the Hot Water Heater.)*

When storing a tank for a long period, best practice is to remove any water decreasing the chances of bacteria causing a problem later.

Water Heater Bypass

No hot water coming out of the faucet but the tank is warm? This indicates that the heater is working. Look for a reason hot water might be rerouted away from the faucet.

A water heater bypass can be the cause of this. A lot of RVs--but not all--have a water heater bypass. Check the valves, do they need to be switched to allow water to flow into the water heater?

Another reason might be that more than one faucet is on at the same time. The water heater system allows cold water to flow over to the hot water side if water is requested in a second location.

Replacing the Anode Rod

New or Reborn   Needs replacing

One of the most important considerations in extending the life of your water heater is whether the anode rod is performing its job--**to divert corrosive action away from the tank walls to the anode rod**.

Salt water also shortens the life of the rod, so if a soft water conditioner is installed, be prepared to replace the rod sooner than normal.

When you smell an offensive odor in the water, it is time to flush the water heater.

If you have a *Suburban* brand of hot water heater, replacing your anode rod at regular intervals may **increase the life of your water heater**, saving you money, time and the inconvenience of having to replace your water heater.

Atwood manufactures a water heater with an aluminum tank that resists corrosion, hence no anode rod necessary. There are some older Atwoods, however, that need an anode rod.

The only way to make sure a rod is needed is to open the drain valve. If one is installed, your water heater needs a rod replacement.

Magnesium, aluminum, or a combination of aluminum, zinc, and tin are the most common elements used to manufacture anode rods. Flexible options for low ceiling clearance or difficult access points are available from your local supply house.

The condition of your anode rod (and whether it is time to replace it) depends upon your water quality, how much the water heater is used, the running temperature, and of course the craftsmanship of the tank itself.

Flushing the Hot Water Heater

This is a simple project, but it does require some strength and a wrench (or other tool) to remove the drain plug. Ask a strong neighbor to help. To complete the flush, purchase a flushing tool (photo below) from any RV store.

To make sure you follow the steps in order, write everything down on a card. After the flush, store the card away for next time.

Option: Soak the tank in white vinegar to better release the mineral residue. Getting the vinegar into the tank through a small drain hole can be tricky. If you have help or a way to attach a long flexible funnel from the drain hole to, say, the awning arm, it might work for you.

1. Turn off the water heater and allow several hours for it to cool. Before you remove the drain plug, run some water from one of your hot faucets to make sure that the water is not hot enough to burn you.

2. Cover the gas burner tube to protect it from the water drain.

3. Turn off the water to the motorhome and remove the drain plug or electric element (*Lightning Rod* or *Hot Rod*).

4. To drain it more quickly, lift the lever of the pressure relief valve. That allows air into the heater and the tank drains much quicker, and it is good to exercise the valve to keep it working properly.

5. *With the drain plug out*, **close the relief valve** and turn city water on to flush out the tank.

6. Install the flushing tool (shown here) to a garden hose and wash the interior of the heater by pointing it downward. This ensures that all solids are flushed from the heater.

7. Continue to use the flushing tool until the water is clear. Once the water comes out clean, allow the water to drain, reinstall the drain plug or heating element, and refill the water heater.

8. Wrap the drain plug threads with Plumber's tape. To secure the drain plug against a possible link, again, ask your strong neighbor for help.

9. Once the heater is filled, run water through a hot water faucet to make sure the air is all out, then turn the heater back on.

10. Store the tools in a plastic bag to keep them clean until time to do this job again next year.

Option: To ensure all the mineral deposits are cleaned out of the tank, add 3 gallons of white vinegar to a 6-gallon tank and set soak for 2 hours minimum, then flush.

Reuse the Anode Rod

You may be able to reuse the anode rod after flushing if you soak it in white vinegar overnight and scrape the mineral deposits off. Steel wool works, along with a sharp blade. Refer to the photo for a comparison.

New or Reborn   *Needs replacing*

NOTES:

Water Pump

 The RV water system consists of a fresh water holding system, plastic or copper water pipes, a 12-volt RV water pump, a gray water tank, and a valve for dumping.

RV water pumps are relatively simple devices. Shurflo, the standard pump manufacturer, probably makes your motorhome's pump. It is powered by 12-volt DC electricity through the inverter, even if you are plugged into a 120-volt AC power.

The RV water pump is an "on demand" system. This means that the pump only kicks on when it is needed. It works by pressurizing your water pipes to a preset PSI (pounds per square inch).

The preset is usually about 30 PSI but most pumps are adjustable. When the power is switched on to the pump, it starts pumping. If any faucets are open, the pump continues to run providing the necessary flow of water.

When you shut the faucet off, the pump continues to run until the preset water pressure builds up in the lines. When this pressure is reached, the pump automatically turns off.

The pressure in the line is maintained until you open a faucet again. When you open the faucet, the pump senses a drop in pressure and begins pumping again.

Some older RV water pumps require you to turn the pump on manually when you want water. Open the faucet, turn the pump on, and water flows out of the faucet. Turn the switch off to the pump and then close the faucet.

The pump switch is on the main Monitor panel inside.

It is important to do things in the right order. These older pumps do not shut off when the water reaches a preset pressure in the line. Leaving the pump running will either overheat the pump or burst a plumbing line.

Pump Not Working

> Check the tank itself to be sure there is actually water in the fresh water holding tank. Believe it or not this is often overlooked.

> It's possible for the water gauges to accumulate residue on them and read full when they are empty.

> Make sure there is power to the pump. Is your RV battery fully charged? If not, can you plug into 120-volt source to make sure you have power?

> There is usually a fuse in the positive wire somewhere near the pump. Check the fuse to see if it is blown. If it is blown, replace it and problem solved.

> Check the connections to the pump.

> If the fuse is good, use a 12-volt test light, or better yet, a multi-meter to check for power at the pump.

> If there are bad spots in the wiring, you need to repair or replace the wiring.

> The switch to the pump failed. Replacing this may be beyond your expertise, so find a local repair service.

> If the pump comes on but does not pump water, it is possible that the diaphragm in the pump has debris in it or it is punctured.

Three screws attach the pump head to the pump casing. Remove these screws and inspect the rubber diaphragm. If damaged, replace it with the repair kit that you can get from the manufacturer.

You can usually buy these at your local RV parts dealer.

> ➤ If the diaphragm looks okay, clean it with a gentle detergent and flush the pump head to remove any debris remaining inside.

> ➤ Check to see that supply line from the fresh water holding tank to the RV water pump is not blocked or punctured. Sometimes there is a shut off valve on this line. Make sure that it is open.

> ➤ If the line is blocked with debris or ice, you need to clear it somehow. Try disconnecting the line at the pump and blow compressed air through the pipe.

> ➤ Be sure and turn the pressure down low on the compressor. You do not want to blow the line and cause a leak. If there is a leak in this supply line, it needs to be repaired or replaced.

> ➤ You may also want to check the connection at the inlet side of the pump to make sure it is not sucking air.

If the **pump does not shut off** there is a leak somewhere in the system. It's either at the outlet connection on the pump, in the plumbing, or at the faucet.

Fresh Water Tank

There are only a few things to know about tanks.

> ❖ If your motorhome ever needs a replacement tank, do not to try to patch it.

> ❖ In freezing conditions, drain or use potable antifreeze to keep the tanks from bursting.

> ❖ Right before you take the first trip in your used motorhome, follow this sanitation procedure below.

❖ If boondocking or storing for a season, sanitize the water system at least once a year.

❖ Reserve 5 to 10 hours to complete the sanitizing task.

❖ Change the internal and external water filters after you finish sanitizing the water system.

❖ Flush out your hot water tank at the same time (see *Flushing the Hot Water Heater*).

Sanitizing the Fresh Water System

1. Drain the water out of the water system; this includes hot water tank, fresh water tank, and the water lines. Close all the drain valves.

   Note: You do not want to start this process with water that is questionable or of unknown quality.

2. Determine the size of your RV water system (the fresh water tank, the hot water tank and 2-3 gallons for water lines depending on the size of your recreation vehicle).

3. Prepare a 5% solution using chlorine bleach (non-scented, non-gel) and water. Example: For a 60-gallon (227 litres) water tank, add 1.5 cups (360 ml) bleach to 6 gallons of water.

4. Add the bleach mixture to the water tank. **Important**: Never pour straight bleach into the RV fresh water tank as this destroys any gaskets along the way.

5. Top up the fresh water tank with water.

6. Run the chlorinated water through all lines (hot and cold one at a time) for one or two minutes. You can smell the chlorine.

7. Top up the fresh water tank with water again.

8. Let the solution soak overnight (a minimum of 4 hours). It is important to allow time for the tank to be properly sanitized.

9. Drain and rinse the water tank and water lines several times with fresh water.

10. To handle the chlorine smell and taste, add a mixture of 1/2 cup of baking soda and a gallon of water to the fresh water tank, repeat the fresh water flush.

Just in case you need to figure out how much water your fresh water tank really holds, here is the formula:

Length x Width x Height divided by 231 equals the Gallons of the Tank.

LxWxH ÷ 231 = Gallons

NOTES:

Refrigerator

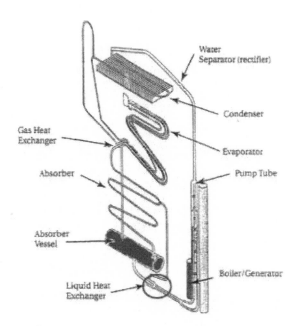

Compared to a household refrigerator, an RV absorption refrigerator cools much slower. The larger the refrigerator, the more efficient. The big plus with the absorption system, besides the "no moving parts," is the quiet operation.

Venting is required to remove the heat generated by the absorption process. A mechanical fan could handle the heat, but is deemed impractical due to the battery drain and the noise level.

What evolved is a complicated absorption system, still the standard equipment today in most RVs. However, larger RVs install household refrigerators apparently without any issues when moving.

RV refrigerators operate by precisely heating a sealed cooling component, with either a gas flame or an electric heating element. The cooling unit amounts to a series of tubes filled with an ammonia-based liquid.

As heat is applied, the fluid circulates through the cooling unit drawing the heat out.

When an RV refrigerator starts failing (not cooling as well), the fluid is no longer circulating properly through the cooling unit.

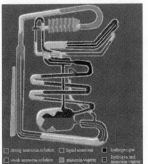

There are no moving parts, no pumps or compressors. The work is done simply by heating liquid. When the ammonia is heated, it circulates.

If the cooling unit develops a leak, the ammonia smell smacks you in the nose. This is not a very common occurrence, but if it does happen, you immediately know where the problem is.

More often, the problem with an RV refrigerator is--time combined with lack of use.

As RV refrigerators age, the ammonia liquid can create sediment that settles to the bottom of the cooling unit. This sediment impedes the ability of the ammonia to circulate properly through the cooling unit. As the sediment builds up, the refrigerator cools less and less.

A refrigerator that is used once or twice a year over a period of 5 or 6 years is much more likely to plug up than one that is always in use.

Things You Can Do to Keep It Cool

Level The Refrigerator

The RV must be fairly level for the refrigerator to operate properly. Older RV refrigerators required more precise leveling, but even newer models must be close to level for optimum performance.

Over time, a cooling unit operated out of level is permanently damaged. When leveling, purchase a small bullseye level and place it in the freezer.

Traveling with the refrigerator operating does not cause problems because the liquids and gases in the cooling unit are constantly moving around.

Unlike an out-of-level stationary refrigerator, liquids do not collect in areas of the cooling unit while on the move.

Pre-cool the Refrigerator

Turn the refrigerator on the day before you plan to leave. When you put in the food, make sure it is already cold. Frozen food should already be frozen.

Putting cold food in the refrigerator, rather than adding warm food, makes for less work for the refrigerator.

One common mistake is to over pack a refrigerator. There must be space between the foods to allow air to circulate throughout the compartment.

Keep a thermometer in the freezer compartment and one in the refrigeration compartment. Check the thermometers frequently to ensure the freezer stays at zero degrees and the refrigerator stays below 40 degrees.

These temperatures may not be possible to sustain in heat over 100 degrees, so be prepared to check food for spoilage.

Installing a vent flue fan helps with this issue (See *Exterior Flue Fans*).

Interior Refrigerator Fan

To help with air circulation, buy an inexpensive, battery operated refrigerator fan. Place the fan in the front part of the refrigerator compartment. It improves the efficiency by circulating the air and reduces the initial cool-down time by half.

Two Alkaline size "D" batteries are required to run the fan and needs replacement after 1-2 months. This fan is well worth the battery expense as it keeps food much fresher, especially salad greens, and reduces the moisture buildup. Put this on your maintenance calendar to check the batteries every two months.

Recommended   *Second choice*

Exterior Flue Fans

If your travel plans include an extended stay in a very hot climate (over 90 degrees F daily), the refrigerator may not stay cool enough to keep food fresh.

Installing a couple of 12 V computer case fans at the top of the refrigerator flue vent eliminates this problem. Depending on the size of your motorhome refrigerator flue, there may only be room for one large fan.

Some refrigerator designs may require the fan to be installed at the bottom; avoid this if possible. Service installers may spin a tale about the best installation, but I have tried both top and bottom vent placement. The top of the vent installation far outperforms the bottom location.

The top vent design is a tougher install project and may cost a few more dollars in labor, but well worth it when the temperature hits 110 degrees. If you understand 12V schematics, it is an easy installation but does require a trip to the roof.

If this seems hazardous for you, check with the park office for a mobile repairperson to do the install.

Measure the top surface opening of the refrigerator flue. Install an on/off switch within easy reach for flexibility in colder climates.

Buy these small computer case fans **yourself** at a local electronics/computer store or online (about $5 each).

Caution: Do not allow the RV repairperson to purchase the fans. They do not usually have the correct specifications or understand the reasoning behind using computer case fans over conventional refrigerator vent fans. Computer fans are also less expensive ($5 versus $35).

Note: Unless your motorhome is less than 20 feet long, ignore the solar-type vent fans; they do not produce enough airflow to do the job.

Minimum specifications to ensure high airflow and low fan noise:

120 mm Computer Case Fan (5 inch):
Air Flow (FM) 44.03; Max. Noise dBA) 23.5

80 mm Computer Case Fan (3 inch):
Air Flow (CFM) 28.89; Max Noise (dBA) 20.9

Routine Refrigerator Maintenance

The heat created by the cooling process is vented behind the refrigerator. Air enters through the outside lower refrigerator vent and attempts to draft the hot air out through the roof vent.

> ➤ Periodically inspect the back of the refrigerator and the roof vent for any obstructions, like bird nests, leaves or other debris that might prevent the heat from escaping.

> ➤ Remove the outside lower vent cover to access the back of the refrigerator. With the refrigerator turned off, make sure connections are clean and tight.

> ➤ Turn the refrigerator on in the LP gas mode and look at the flame. If burning poorly, or is yellow-colored, or if the refrigerator is not operating properly in the gas mode, it is possible that the baffle inside the flue is covered with soot.

> ➤ Clean the burner assembly (Liquid Heat Exchanger) with a pipe cleaner.

> ➤ Turn the refrigerator off again and locate the burner. Directly above the burner is the flue. The baffle is inside the flue. Wear a pair of safety glasses and use an air compressor to blow air up into the flue.

> ➤ After the flue is clean, use the compressed air to remove any debris from the outside refrigerator compartment.

> ➤ Turn the refrigerator on in the LP gas mode to make sure it is working properly. The bright blue flame indicates all is well.

Road vibrations loosen deposits allowing them to crumble and fall to the burner. The finer particles fall into the burner itself, while the larger pieces stay on top of the burner and cause problems with the flame sensor.

As the fine particles build up inside the burner, they create problems with the flame and reduce the heat output of the burner. Pull out the orifice and soak it in rubbing alcohol, then allow it to air dry.

If you cannot get it clean, just replace it, not the whole refrigerator or cooling unit! For a thorough cleaning of the flue and baffle, it may necessary to have an RV dealer do it for you.

While in for service, schedule an LP gas pressure test too.

Refrigerator Not Working

There are a number of reasons that a refrigerator stops working; typically those problems can be repaired at a reasonable cost.

Propane Gas Does Not Ignite

This sounds silly, but check to make sure that the outside propane tank is turned ON. Simple solutions are the best.

Pilot Light

If the pilot light does not stay lit, you may have a bad thermocouple that controls gas flow.

Electronic Ignition

If your electronic ignition fails to light, you may have a faulty control board.

Works on Gas Only

If your refrigerator works on gas, but does not work on electric, you may have a burned out heating element.

If any of these problems exist for you, have a qualified technician check it out. This is not something you can fix without experience in this field.

A word to the wise, if the problem lies in the cooling unit, you may be better off buying a new RV refrigerator instead of repairing your old one.

The high cost of repair is the labor taking the old refrigerator out, taking it apart and putting it back together, then re-installing it; usually an all day job. A new one is installed in about an hour.

Absorber Cool, Boiler Section Hot

If your refrigerator is not staying cool, check the absorber. Is it cool, and the boiler section hot? (See *Routine Refrigerator Maintenance* for diagram.)

This is relatively easy to check, but to get the most accurate reading of the cooler temperature, stick a thermometer in a glass of water (necessary to equalize the temperature) and put it in the refrigerator.

After 12 hours, the temperature should be no higher than 43 degrees F. After 24 hours, it should be in the low 20's to high 30's maximum.

If you cannot maintain these temperatures, the cooling unit is bad. The unit can be replaced, rebuilt, or the entire refrigerator replaced. If this is happening in very hot weather, see *Exterior Flue Fans* before making a decision.

However, the first thing to be checked is the level of the refrigerator. Propane-style refrigerators must be level or they do not work properly. This is the easy solution, and it could save you a lot of money.

Boondocking Tips

If you boondock a lot you may be interested to know how much propane your refrigerator uses. As discussed earlier, it is important to keep an eye on the monitor, or the manual gauge on the outside tank.

If you have a 12 cu/ft Norcold refrigerator that burns 2400 BTU/hr., one gallon of propane lasts about 38 hrs. However, that applies only if the refrigerator runs constantly. Again, assuming it runs for 8 hours out of a 24 hr. period, a gallon of propane lasts about 5 days.

The total amount depends on outside temperature, how full the refrigerator along with the temperature setting, and how often you open the door. If you have a 30-gallon propane tank, it should last about 150 days.

Climate Control Feature Drains Battery

Some refrigerators have a "high humidity" switch, or equivalent, usually located in the freezer doorframe that attaches to a small heater element. It controls the humidity that may collect around the door opening during very high humidity situations.

This circuit draws about 6 Amps and drains a battery in less than 12 hours. An easy solution: Flip the switch to the "off" position when you are running the refrigerator on battery power.

Furnace

Many travelers seem destined to wind up in cold places, not always by choice. The furnace becomes an important part of their lives. It is noisy, burns lots of propane, and generates soot. If it is not working, however, the scenario can be life-threatening. It is wise to understand the basics.

❖ What is a BTU? 1 BTU equals the heat energy required to raise the temperature of 1 pound of water by 1 degree. To calculate the BTU rating:
Total sq. ft. of RV x 125 = BTU needed.

❖ The motorhome furnace fan is powered by the 12 VDC system. When boondocking, the furnace ignites and burns through propane at a rapid rate. It does cycle on and off with the thermostat.

❖ After turning on the furnace, wait for about 15 to 30 seconds for the furnace blower to start. This is usually a very loud sound, so be prepared. The air coming from the blower is cold at this point.

❖ The burner ignites after the blower starts.

❖ Using the thermostat, the blower and burner cycle on and off depending on the temperature setting. The burner shuts down first, with the blower some seconds later.

❖ Five gallons of propane (20 lb. tank) should last for roughly 18 hours.

❖ A furnace with a rating of 26,000 BTUH consumes 1 gallon of liquid propane every 3.5 hours.

Furnace Not Working or Operating Correctly

➤ If your furnace refuses to operate, check the wall mounted thermostat switch. Ensure that the ON/OFF switch is in the ON position.

➤ Look for a wasp nest located in the vent on one side of the motorhome. Mice and other critters can also build nests inside.

➤ A rumor circulating the RV communities states that placing LED rope lights around the bottom of the motorhome 24x7 keeps critters out. You might try this.

➤ If the gas pressure is not at 11.00 W.C. the furnace works inconsistently and crates unbalanced combustion. Get a qualified propane technician to complete a Manometer test to determine that the proper LPG pressure of 11.00 W.C. exists for furnace use.

➤ A simple pressure-drop test can determine if there is a gas leak. Any mobile repairperson can do this.

➤ Be careful not to cover or restrict the heater ducts. Pressure backup causes the furnace to malfunction.

➤ Check the air intake and flue areas of the furnace for obstructions caused by critter nests.

➤ Use a multimeter to test that the DC voltage is between 10.5 and 13.5 VDC at the furnace during operation. Low voltage can cause the furnace to overheat. Check the battery monitor for starting voltage. If the voltage is in the range, then the problem lies at the furnace.

➤ Check for a tripped circuit breaker. Another reason to always check the "line monitor" to ensure that the polarity is correct. (See *Managing Power*.)

➤ If the blower runs but fails to ignite, check the air intake for restrictions.

Filtering Your Water

Almost every location in the USA suffers from polluted water. To maintain a healthy lifestyle *filter all water coming into* the motorhome.

Exterior Water Filter

The best exterior water filter systems feature a sturdy house-quality canister (usually blue opaque) with a coarse filter to take out the heavy materials. A carbon filter canister can be daisy-chained to the primary filter by using a brass male-to-male or female-to-female hose adapter.

Connect these canisters to your drinking water hose that fastens to the main park water source.

These filters do not remove anything but sediment and chlorine (if using the carbon filter too).

Hardware stores often carry this blue canister. Designed for pipe water transfer, make sure you get the adapters for "pipe to hose." One male-to-female, and one female-to-male are necessary to hook up to the water hoses at your site. Two "for drinking water only" hoses are required (see *Drinking Water Hoses and Connectors*).

Drinking Water Filters

For drinking water, install a *Reverse Osmosis water filter system* under your kitchen sink cabinet, or under the dinette seat. The Reverse Osmosis process eliminates bacteria, fluoride, and chlorine.

 There are several RO designs available, but I recommend a two-gallon storage tank with a four-filter system: carbon, pre-filter, osmosis unit, and the small final filter to take out any storage tank taste or smell.

Order these systems online or through a local water store. Installation can be done by most park-recommended vendors, a local water store, or yourself.

It is a fairly simply installation, you just need to make sure that the hoses are connected properly, no power required.

It takes at least 40-psi water pressure (the standard for most RV parks) to make the filters effective. If you have reason to doubt the park pressure level, buy a water pressure hose gauge at your local hardware store, or online.

To install the separate drinking water faucet, a hole saw tough enough to penetrate stainless steel or porcelain is needed. If the sink is too small, a countertop can be used.

For complete information on how reverse-osmosis systems work, visit:

science.howstuffworks.com/reverse-osmosis.htm

Drinking Water Hoses and Connectors

Drinking
Water Hose
5/8 inch

Male-to-Male Adapter   Female-to-Female Adapter

5/8 x 25 feet
5/8 x 10 feet
5/8 x 04 feet

Carry a male-to-male and a female-to-female drinking water hose *adapter* in the outside compartment where you keep the water hoses. Keep the adapters in the bin with your 4-foot, 10-foot, and 25-foot drinking water hoses.

If you use the blue filter cartridge as mentioned in the *Exterior Water Filter* section, add the "pipe-to-hose" connectors to the bin as well.

Often park water connections are not standard, so be prepared. Include a small supply of different size hose gaskets to handle the hose connection leaks that occur without warning.

Water Purity Tester

One tool I find very useful is a water purity tester. The *IntelliTEC Water Quality Tester* I purchased is more accurate that those expensive test strips. It is reasonable priced and has an off/on button and a "read" button so you can read the results after removing the tester.

If the TSDs (total dissolved solids) are over 200, do not drink the water.

Extra TV Cable

Bring 15 to 25 feet of extra RG6 cable as an extension for your high-definition flat-screen TV. It pays to be flexible. RV parks may place their cable receptacle in hard to reach locations. If carrying a portable high-definition satellite TV dish with you, the extra cable may be necessary. Include a couple of barrel connectors (small round adapters that connect two coaxial "F" connectors together) in this kit.

You may find that the original internal coaxial cable (probably RG58) in your motorhome does not make a good connection to your new high-definition flat screen TV. Instead of having the entire motorhome rewired with RG6 (very expensive), run your extra cable from the park receptacle through a window directly to the back of the TV.

Make sure that the pins within the "F" connectors at each end are inserted properly and tightened. If problems occur, look for a bent pin in the connector.

Towing Your Car

To tow or not to tow is a major decision for most motorhome travelers. Take the first short trip without a tow in place, and then make the decision after returning.

The cost of fuel, the inconvenience of hooking and unhooking the tow, the lack of transportation at your destination, and road safety are the topics usually discussed on this issue.

Not towing any vehicle behind the motorhome:

Upside: More flexibility for the driver; no increased fuel cost

Downside: Hassle of finding a rental auto for touring

The tow equipment on the back of the motorhome is heavy to lift when adjusting but not outside most women's capabilities. Hooking up and unhooking takes time and is sometimes frustrating.

Most travelers find a toad worthwhile for the convenience of having a touring car.

Without a tow car, it is possible to hire someone in the RV park to shuttle you to the grocery store. However, if you like to explore museums and tourist attractions, this might get cumbersome. In you are in a metro area, hiring a taxi is a viable option. Some parks actually have cars for hire.

If you choose the car option, ensure that your "toad" can travel "wheels-down." Wheels-down means that all four wheels touch the road while towing.

The expense can be around $1,000+ for both vehicles. It is best to find a vendor that is familiar with your car and towing hardware to get the best installation.

Tow Wheels-Down

Not every automobile can be towed wheels-down. Do your research on this; your current auto may not be designed for towing. I do not recommend a car dolly. These are hard to manage, heavy to move by hand and store once at the destination. However, it may be the only option for you.

Here is a website to explore for information:

www.blueox.us/instruction/towingbasics101.htm

Pay close attention to the auto weight as well as the towability. If buying a high-powered diesel motorhome, the toad options are many. On the other hand, a small gas-powered rig has severe limitations on its pulling power.

Try to stay under 4,000 pounds if possible. Traveling up and down hills or mountains can create a severe strain on the engine, hence the lighter weight. You may also need additional braking power.

Any tow vehicle is going to get some exterior damage from rocks and debris. When traveling I use a padded vinyl front cover for my Honda CR-V. It extends above the windshield and fastens to the doors and wheel wells.

When towing, be prepared to have a problem now and then detaching the car from the tow bar. Best practice is to unhook on a flat straight surface.

If you decide to unhook the toad while the motorhome is at an odd angle, the safety pins on the tow bar may jam. I keep a rubber mallet and a 12-inch spike with a flat end in my toolkit to dislodge the pins.

Motorhome Tires

Take the motorhome in for service before you start on your first trip and ask the technician to check the tire pressure and note any bumps, checks, or slits in all four/six tires.

 The technician can find the "tire date" for you. The date is located in the embossed area where other information is stored. If not located, check the "inside" of the tire.

Write this date down on your *"My Motorhome Components"* sheet for future reference. Download this components sheet from my webpage:

TheRVLifestyle.MovingOnWithMargo.com#mh.

When replacing tires, try to get all replacements stamped with the same date code. This date should be as close to the purchase date as possible. This ensures that they all came from the same manufacturing batch and should be evenly balanced on the road with lots of life left on the sidewalls.

Michelin recommends "any tires in service 10 years or more from the date of manufacture, including spare tires, be replaced with new tires as a simple precaution even if such tires appear serviceable and even if they have not reached the legal wear limit."

❖ If the cracks are less than 1/32" deep, the tire is okay. to run.

❖ Between 1/32" and 2/32", the tire is suspect and should be examined by your tire dealer.

❖ If the cracks are over 2/32, replace immediately.

Wear bars, narrow strips of smooth rubber across the tread, appear when $2/32^{nd}$ of an inch of tread remains. Replace the tire immediately.

Keeping proper tire pressure is one of best ways to help tires last longer. Follow the psi pressure listed on the tire itself, not from other sources.

The only portable air compressors small enough to travel with you do not have enough power to pump up a motorhome tire. Even those compressors that claim to have up to 120 psi rarely prove to be powerful enough.

That means relying on tire or repair shops. When taking the motorhome in for an oil change, insist that they check the tire for cuts, checks, and tread depth.

Find out the correct psi by looking directly on the tire and make sure they write it down on the order form. The pressure psi listed on the tire is not a recommendation, but a maximum that should not be exceeded.

After cleaning the motorhome tires with soap and water, apply a non-petroleum-based product like *303 Aerospace Protectant*. As far as I know, this is the only product that works as advertised in combating UV damage.

Another thing to consider is the fact that any tire dressing that contains petroleum products, alcohol, and/or silicone materials may further damage the tire due to a possible chemical reaction with the antioxidant material in the tire.

Most owners cover the tires when spending more than a few days in one location. There are vinyl covers available at any RV store. However, it is a dirty job to cover and uncover the tires as the vinyl tends to pick up dirt and insects just like the tires.

The latest tire cover option is shade cloth. The most effective way is to install snap or twist fasteners around the wheel wells. It is easy to remove and store the shade.

Look at this vendor's product to understand how it works then find a local vendor to sell and install the shades:

www.rvsungard.com/tire-savers

Rotation and Alignment

The consensus among RV tire experts online is to rotate the tires only if you see irregular wear patterns on the front tires. This might also indicate an alignment is necessary.

Personally, I had an alignment done as soon as I bought my used motorhome, and the tires rotated according to my chassis manufacturer's instructions (important). My tires are wearing well to this day, several years later.

If you put 10,000 miles a year on your motorhome, the tires are probably going to be replaced before you need to have them rotated. Although, having an alignment done even with a new motorhome is a good idea; today's quality control is not rigorous.

Hydraulic Leveling Systems

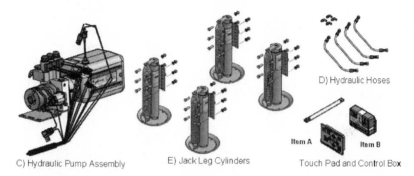

C) Hydraulic Pump Assembly   E) Jack Leg Cylinders

D) Hydraulic Hoses

Item A   Item B

Touch Pad and Control Box

Choosing a motorhome with a hydraulic leveling system eliminates the hassle of using leveling blocks under all the wheels. Since the refrigerator needs to be level to work properly, the leveling ritual becomes a priority when arriving at our destination.

Walk around the motorhome to determine the soil content. If the ground looks or feels soft, use leveling blocks under the jack pads. This is especially important if the motorhome is over 32 feet and diesel-powered (heavy), as the pads can dig large holes in the ground.

The leveler control panel is next to the steering wheel. When extending any of the jacks, a noisy bong sounds until shut off. When retracting, the bong continues until all jacks are docked. Learn the shifting sounds of the bong to help you figure out the progress. With older motorhomes, visually check that the levelers are docked. If not, service the system.

Maintenance Procedures

The hydraulic levelers require some maintenance.

> ➢ A careful maintenance check twice a year should be enough to keep the system running smoothly. Run the hydraulic jacks up and down about six times to lubricate them.

> ➢ If you notice that one or more of the levelers do not fully retract or extend, maintenance is suggested.

> ➢ Check the reservoir with the jacks (and any slideout) in the **fully retracted** position. The fluid should be $\frac{3}{4}$ inches into the dipstick (if provided) or to the bottom of the fill port.

> ➢ Most systems use Type A Automatic Transmission Fluid (Dexron, ATF) to refill the reservoir; other systems use hydraulic fluid. Check your documentation. Do not mix the fluids.

> ➢ A few systems need to have the fluid changed every 24 months. Check your documentation.

> ➢ The location of the reservoir varies with the model of the motorhome. Often in gas-driven models, the reservoir is in the front near the oil reservoir.

> ➢ Inspect and clean all hydraulic pump electrical connections every 12 months.

> ➢ Remove dirt and road debris from jacks as needed.

> ➢ If jacks are down for extended periods, spray the exposed leveling jack chrome rods with a silicone lubricant every month for protection against the elements.

> ➢ Do not use a greasy lubricant (such as Lithium) to maintain the seal on the bottom of the jack cylinder. This type of lubricant attracts and holds gravel and dirt. Use a light weight lubricant spray.

Other Maintenance Areas

Wheel Bearings

With annual lubrication and proper care, a wheel bearing can last for many years. Have the bearings checked with each service, repacked when necessary.

If purchasing a used motorhome, checking the wheel bearings are at the top of the list. You may need to have the bearings repacked.

Axels, Brakes, Differential

All axels should be checked once a year. Brakes should be checked with each tire inspection, if possible. Pay particular attention when traveling near salty air, as brakes suck in the caustic air. This applies to driving on snow-plowed roads too.

Every few years service the differential (if applicable).

Engine Transmission

The transmission should be flushed every 30,000 miles, but the fluids are checked every time the oil is changed.

Engine Belts and Hoses

After purchasing a used motorhome, have all the belts and hoses checked immediately, along with an oil change and lube. Checking the belts and hoses should also be on the **pre-purchase checklist**.

After retrieving from storage, always check the belts and hoses, just in case some critter has made their home inside the compartment.

Motorhome Slideouts

If your motorhome has slideouts, there are several functions to be aware of when retracting and extending them:

> ➢ Always follow the manufacturer's instructions regarding the leveling of the coach.

> ➢ If the coach is equipped with a luggage compartment beneath the room that extends, make sure the compartment doors are closed so not to interfere with the slide out operation.

> ➢ Check for obstacles or people both inside and outside the vehicle.

> ➢ Make sure all pins and bars have been removed and no obstructions visible on the inside walls or floor.

> ➢ Set the Park Brake.

> ➢ To check the hydraulic fluid, fully retract all slides. Remove the breather cap from the top of the hydraulic oil reservoir. The oil level should be approximately one inch below the top of the reservoir.

> ➢ See the manufacturer's instructions for the proper fluid to refill the reservoir.

> ➢ In an emergency, Dexron Automatic Transmission Fluid can be used. Do not use brake fluid or hydraulic jack fluid.

> ➢ Treat outer seals occasionally with *303 Protectant* for a smooth quiet operation.

> ➢ To avoid vinyl flooring scratches or carpet pile snags, clean the floors inside before retracting.

Hot Weather Tips

Refrigerator

Simple Maintenance

When it is hot outside, try parking your RV with the refrigerator side in the shade. Periodically inspect and clean the refrigerator door gaskets.

To check the doors for a good seal:

> ➢ Place a dollar bill behind the seal and close the door. It should stay there and not drop.

> ➢ When you try to pull it out there should be some resistance. Do this in several different places and have any damaged seals replaced.

Install Exterior Flue Fans

If your travel plans include an extended stay in a very hot climate (over 90 degrees F daily), the refrigerator may not stay cool enough to keep food fresh.

 Installing a couple of 12 V computer case fans at the top of the refrigerator vent helps eliminate this problem. Depending on the size of your motorhome, there may only be room for one large fan.

Some refrigerator designs may require the fan to be installed at the bottom; avoid this if possible.

Some installers may spin a tale about the best installation, but I have tried both top and bottom vent installs and find the fans installed in the top of the vent by far outperforms the bottom location.

The top vent design is a tougher install project and may cost a few more dollars in labor, but well worth it when the temperature hits 110 degrees.

Purchase these small computer case fans at a local electronics/computer store or online (about $5 each). Install it yourself or contact a local RV repairperson to install the fans at your RV park site. Install an on/off switch for flexibility in colder climates.

Minimum specifications to ensure high airflow and low fan noise:

120 mm Computer Case Fan (5 inch):
Air Flow (FM) 44.03; Max. Noise dBA) 23.5

80 mm Computer Case Fan (3 inch):
Air Flow (CFM) 28.89; Max Noise (dBA) 20.9

Interior Wood Cabinets

During hot weather, leave the cabinet doors ajar to ensure ventilation and reduce warping.

Window Shields

To maintain cooler temperatures inside the motorhome, purchase sun shades for the windows.

Although exterior sun shades are somewhat efficient, they are expensive and time-consuming to attach and store. You must climb a ladder and installing requires more strength than most of us have to stretch them across the windshield.

Storing Your motorhome

Drain the Tanks

➢ Remove the drain plug on the water heater. Allow the water to drain out. Replace the plug.

➢ Find the drain plug on the water tank. Drain all but a few gallons. Replace the plug.

➢ Use potable Antifreeze in the fresh water tank to prevent freezing.

Water Pump

➢ Run the water pump until it sucks air.

➢ Using *potable* Anti-freeze in the fresh water tank should prevent any problems in the lines.

Avoid Broken Pipes

Keep water in the pipes P-trap. Each month while in storage, add a little water to the pipes.

Gray and Black Water Tanks

Keep a small amount of water in each tank. Pump a small amount of *potable* antifreeze into each tank.

Generator

Run the generator for at least **30 minutes every three months**. Every 50 hours, check the spark plugs. Change the oil and filter.

Tires

> ➤ Place cardboard, plastic, or plywood between the tire and the storage surface.
> ➤ Store out of a high ozone area.
> ➤ Cover the tires, if stored in direct sunlight.
> ➤ Lower the hydraulic levelers to take some of the weight off the tires.

Refrigerator

> ➤ Leave an open container of baking soda inside to absorb odors.
> ➤ Prop the door open a few inches.

Windows

> ➤ Close all blinds and curtains.
> ➤ Use reflective coverings inside the windows.

Vents

> ➤ Leave one vent cracked for air circulation. Depending on the storage environment, close all other openings.
> ➤ Cover the furnace vent and hot water vents with protective screens to keep out the critters.
> ➤ Close any other openings inside with rags or foam that might allow critters to enter.

Miscellaneous Items

The temperature inside a stored motorhome can fluctuate wildly. Expect any item stored to be affected. Remove everything pressurized, canned, or liquid.

Driving Tips

Proper Braking Technique

The use of brakes on a long and/or steep downgrade is only a supplement to the braking effect of the engine. Here is a tip courtesy of *Escapee Magazine*.

1. When your speed increases to or above your safe speed, apply the brakes aggressively enough to feel a definite slowdown.

2. When your speed is reduced to approximately five (5) mph below your safe speed, release the brake. It should take about 3 seconds on the brake pedal to do this.

3. When your speed increases again to your safe speed, repeat steps 1 and 2.

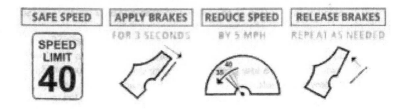

If your motorhome is gas powered, this information should help ease the tension on grades. It is usually a long, slow, haul up and a slightly scary ride down.

Understanding the Gears

If in a gas-powered motorhome, watch the speed to determine when to shift on grades.

Most Chevrolet and Ford engines have four forward gears:

Automatic Overdrive – Normal driving without grades. When passing another vehicle at less than 35 mph, push the accelerator pedal half-way to the floor. If passing at more than 35 mph, push the pedal all the way to the floor.

D for 3rd Gear – Normal driving with some steep hills. This gear can be used instead of Overdrive, but the gas consumption is greater.

2nd Gear – Used for steep grades or slow speeds for control. Do not exceed 40 mph in this gear.

1st Gear – Used for very slow speeds for control or torque. Do not exceed 30 mph.

The rule for choosing gears on grades is to use the same gear going down as when climbing. Use your best judgment. It is important to select the proper gear before starting the downgrade. You may find it impossible to down shift at high speeds.

Understand that the engine is going to make a loud surging sound when changing to a lower gear. This is normal and indicates that all is well. If you watch the RPMs, note that the engine sound changes as the RPMs increase.

According to online sources, the 2500 to 3500 RPM range is the happy place for most gas-powered engines. This means that if the RPMs drop into the lower range, the engine is getting more wear than necessary.

Adjusting Outside Mirrors

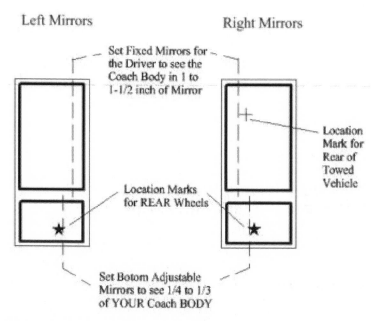

Courtesy of Don Bobbitt

Adjusting the large side mirrors on your motorhome is similar to your car. The difference is that the motorhome has broken the scene in the mirror down into two pieces.

The top mirror looks down the side of the motorhome (just like in your car), but the bottom mirror looks down to the road and back, so you can see your rear wheels.

The bottom mirror also allows you to see any auto coming up alongside into what would be your blind spot.

Backing with the Stars

In the illustration above, note the stars in the bottom mirrors. These stars are very helpful markers when backing into a site.

To mark your mirror: Have someone stand at the rear wheel well. Place the star on the bottom mirror where their knees are reflected. Repeat this on the other side or use the awning arm (if over the wheel well).

Pivot Point When Turning

The pivot point is in the center of the rear axle. This is an important point to recognize so you can see how the motorhome rotates around a turn. If any stationary object, like a tree, is at the center of the rear axle, you do not hit it when you turn.

Tail Swing

Tail swing is the distance that the body of the motorhome, behind the pivot point, moves in the opposite direction of the front when turning.

To measure the swing distance, stop the motorhome along a straight line. Make a complete turn away from the line. Have someone measure the maximum swing as you turn.

An excellent time to do this measurement is during your RV driving class. Have the instructor measure the swing for you. Part of a driving class curriculum is to help you judge when to setup to start a backing turn.

Cargo Weight Balance

One of the major causes of accidents with recreational vehicles of any kind is the weight imbalance. It is very important to get the motorhome weighed soon.

A few commercial scales allow RVs to weigh the front and back separately. A fee may be charged.

Before you can get the feel of how much stopping time is necessary, you must understand the weight balance.

You already have experienced items that become projectiles when thrown. These are now stowed. The next step is getting the feel of the weight distribution in the cabinets and outside compartments.

When the levelers are extended, if you always extend one side more than the other, this is a sign of weight imbalance.

> ➤ Get the motorhome weighed as soon as possible. Pull into the nearest commercial highway scales station; visit a major RV rally and look for a vendor; call around to truck repair shops (or check the yellow pages) to find the nearest scale.

> ➤ Fix any imbalance by shifting something as innocent as canned goods, sporting goods, heavy dinnerware...you get the picture.

Motorhome manufacturers are supposed to put weight balance at the top of the list when they design the interior. The chassis is rated for the maximum load.

This is expressed in the following cryptic symbols, courtesy of the *RV Safety & Education Foundation*:

GVWR

Gross Vehicle Weight Rating is the *maximum* allowable weight of the fully loading vehicle, including liquids, passengers, cargo, and the tongue weight of any towed vehicle.

GAWR

Gross Axel Weight Rating is the *maximum* allowable weight each axle assembly is designed to carry, measured at the tires. This includes the weight of the axle assembly (tires, wheels, springs, axle).

This rating assumes that the load is equal on each side. It is also established by rating the axle assembly on the weakest link.

GCWR

Gross Combination Weight Rating is the *maximum allowable combined weight* of the tow vehicle and the attached towed vehicle. This rating assumes that both vehicles have functioning brakes.

GTWR

Gross Trailer Weight Rating is the *maximum* towed vehicle weight. Each component (receiver, drawbar, ball) of a ball-type hitch has its own rating.

TWR/TLR/LR

Tongue Weight, Tongue Load, and **Vertical Load Rating** are different terms for the *maximum vertical load* that can be carried by the hitch.

Tire Ratings

The *maximum* load that a tire may carry is engraved on the sidewall, along with a corresponding cold inflation pressure. A reduction in inflation pressure requires a reduction in load rating. In other words, keep the motorhome tires as the highest maximum psi allowed.

UVW

Unloaded Vehicle is the weight of a vehicle as built at the factory with full fuel, engine/generator oil and coolants. It *does not include* cargo, fresh water, LP gas, occupants, or dealer installed accessories.

NCC

Net Carrying is the *maximum* weight of all personal belongings, food, fresh water, LP gas, tools, and dealer installed accessories that can be carried by the RV.

SCWR

Sleeping Capacity Weight Rating is the manufacturers designated *number of sleeping positions* multiplied by 154 pounds (70 kilograms).

CCC

Cargo Carrying Capacity is equal to **GVWR minus** each of the following: **UVW**, full fresh potable water weight (including the water in the water heater), full LP gas weight, and **SCWR**.

Liquid Weights (Pounds Per Gallon)

- ❖ • Water: 8.3
- ❖ • Gasoline: 5.6
- ❖ • Diesel Fuel: 6.8
- ❖ • Propane: 4.2 at 60 degrees F (expanding at 1.5 percent per ten degrees Fahrenheit)

Follow Margo's blog: **MovingOnWithMargo.com**

Other eBooks by Margo Armstrong

RV LIFESTYLE SERIES

* For Women Only - Traveling Solo In Your RV

* For Women Only – Motorhome Care & Maintenance

* How To Save Money While Enjoying The RV Lifestyle

* The RV Lifestyle - A Dream Come True

* Selling Online - Supporting the Traveling Lifestyle

* Staying In Touch, A Traveler's Guide

* Working On The Road

WRITING BOOKS

* Writing & Publishing Books for Fun & Profit

38643751R00071